National Credit Union Administration

Federal Credit Union Handbook

Prepared by the
Office of Examination and Insurance

NCUA-8055 (Rev 2006) M-4035

Table of Contents

Foreword		4
Preface		5
Part I	Federal Credit Unions	7
Part II	Organizational Structure and Control	13
Part III	Member Services	21
Part IV	Operational Requirements	27
Part V	Management	31
Part VI	NCUA Funds and Programs	45
Part VII	Other Laws Affecting Federal Credit Unions	49
Part VIII	Conflict of Interest	61
Part IX	Other Procedures and Supplemental Information	65

Foreword

The *Federal Credit Union Handbook* was created to assist the board of directors in conducting the credit union's affairs. The Handbook covers a wide range of subjects and is intended as a general reference. However, the contents should prove useful to credit union officials and employees in carrying out their duties and responsibilities.

We encourage credit union officials to become familiar with other National Credit Union Administration publications, laws, and regulations.

Preface

In the early twentieth century, credit needs of the urban working classes in the United States were largely neglected by established financial institutions. For the most part, the average worker had nowhere to turn except to the usurious money lenders of the day. This growing dependency complicated the economic life of the average consumer and gave rise to the development and formation of a cooperative credit system in the United States, an idea originating in Europe and imported to North America in 1900. In 1908, the first legally chartered cooperative credit society was established in Manchester, New Hampshire by a special act of the state's legislature. The following year, the first complete credit union act, the *Massachusetts Credit Union Act*, became law in Massachusetts. By 1933, enactment of state laws permitting formation of credit unions had been largely accomplished. In 1934, the *Federal Credit Union Act* was signed into law, giving further impetus to the movement.

The post World War II era gave rise to an enormous appetite for consumer goods and an attendant need for consumer credit. Credit unions met this need to an increasing extent and expanded rapidly. The credit union system became a recognized social and economic force in the United States. By the end of 2003, over 82.4 million people were members of credit unions.

Credit unions differ from other financial institutions in that they are cooperative associations organized to serve members with a common bond of employment, association, or residence. Another characteristic that sets them apart is volunteerism. The founders of the movement believed volunteers should direct the organization and operation of credit unions.

Credit unions are organized under a dual-chartering system of federal and state laws. Federal and state chartered credit unions purposes include promoting thrift among their members and creating a source of credit at reasonable interest rates.

Part I
Federal Credit Unions

A federal credit union is a not-for-profit financial institution cooperative organized to provide its members with a place to save and a source of loans at reasonable rates. It is a corporation chartered under the *Federal Credit Union Act* to serve groups having a common bond of occupation or association, or groups within a well-defined, local neighborhood, community, or rural district. More information about federal credit union organization and the chartering policies of the National Credit Union Administration (NCUA) may be obtained from NCUA's regional offices.

The Federal Credit Union Act

The *Federal Credit Union Act* provides for the chartering and supervising of federal credit unions by NCUA and the insuring of member accounts of federal and state-chartered credit unions through the National Credit Union Share Insurance Fund (NCUSIF).

Section 107 of the *Federal Credit Union Act* specifically defines a federal credit union's direct (express) powers. The following provides three examples of direct power: The power to accept share deposits, the power to make loans to members, and the power to borrow funds.

Section 107 of the *Federal Credit Union Act* also grants indirect (incidental) powers to a federal credit union. These powers are necessary to enable a federal credit union to carry out the business for which it was chartered. Since the *Federal Credit Union Act* does not specifically define incidental powers, the board of directors should ensure any activity not specifically authorized by the Act or by Part 721 of *NCUA Rules and Regulations*, is clearly within the credit union's indirect powers. If the board of directors has any questions with respect to the proposed activity, it should seek an advisory opinion from NCUA General Counsel or consult with the appropriate NCUA Regional Director.

Since 1934, various amendments to the *Federal Credit Union Act* have greatly expanded the ability of federal credit unions to meet their members' financial needs; however, the basic purposes of a federal credit union, as stated in the Act, remain unchanged.

National Credit Union Administration (NCUA)

The National Credit Union Administration is in the Executive Branch of the Federal Government. NCUA receives no appropriations and operates solely from monies received from insured credit unions. NCUA is headquartered in Alexandria, Virginia, but it operates on a decentralized basis through five regional offices which are located in Albany, New York; Alexandria, Virginia; Atlanta, Georgia; Austin, Texas; and Tempe, Arizona. More than 80 percent of the Agency's employees are assigned to the regions. Each regional office is managed by a regional director who reports to the Executive Director. The NCUA Board consists of a Chairman and two Board Members, each appointed by the President and confirmed by the Senate. The NCUA Board and its headquarters staff provide policy, direction, and administrative support to the regional offices.

NCUA Objectives

NCUA's activities are predicated on four objectives which support the mission to ensure a stable and cooperative credit union system. NCUA's four objectives consist of the following:

- To ensure the safety and soundness of the credit union system.
- To foster cooperation between credit unions and NCUA (the regulator/ insurer).
- To improve the efficiency and the effectiveness of NCUA's supervision including reducing the regulatory burden.
- To ensure fair and equal access of financial services for all Americans.

NCUA Rules and Regulations

Under authority of the *Federal Credit Union Act*, NCUA prescribes rules and regulations for the organization and operation of federal credit unions. All rules and regulations are published in the *National Credit Union Administration Rules and Regulations*.

It is NCUA's policy to ensure its regulations impose only minimal burdens on credit unions, consumers, and the public. No major regulatory changes are made without first affording federally insured credit unions and other interested persons the opportunity to comment. Credit union officials are encouraged to participate in the regulatory process and submit their comments to NCUA. For further information about the Agency's policies for the promulgation of rules, refer to *NCUA Interpretive Ruling and Policy Statement (IRPS) No. 03-02* dated May 29, 2003.

Charter

After an organization certificate, filed by the subscribers of a proposed federal credit union, is approved by NCUA; the document becomes the credit union's official charter. Among other things, the charter includes the credit union's official name and also defines the field of membership.

From time to time, a federal credit union may find it necessary to make changes to its name or field of membership, this action requires an application requesting an amendment to the charter. Applications for amendments should be made to the regional director via the US Mail or the Internet. For additional information pertaining to charter amendment procedures, please contact the appropriate regional offices or refer to *NCUA's Chartering and Field of Membership Manual (NCUA 8007)*.

Bylaws

NCUA prescribes standard *Federal Credit Union Bylaws (NCUA 8001)* for adoption upon chartering. Once adopted by the board of directors, the standard Bylaws become the official Bylaws of the credit union.

Standard bylaw amendments may be adopted by the board of directors without further NCUA approval. Applications for approval of non-standard amendments should be forwarded to the appropriate regional director for consideration. For further information, refer to the *Federal Credit Union Standard Bylaws (NCUA 8001A)*.

NCUA Letters, Regulatory Alerts, Interpretive Rulings, and Accounting Bulletins

NCUA publishes numbered Letters to Credit Unions, Opinion Letters, Regulatory Alerts, Interpretive Rulings and Policy Statements, and Accounting

Bulletins. These documents discuss a variety of topics of interest and should be retained in the permanent files for ready reference.

Examinations

The principal method by which NCUA carries out its supervisory responsibility is through on-site risk-focused examinations. These examinations are designed to determine the risk to the NCUA Share Insurance Fund. The examiner's review focuses on management's ability to identify, measure, monitor, and control risk.

Throughout the exam, it is essential for credit union officials and employees to cooperate fully. This includes making the credit union's books and records readily available to the examiner. To facilitate an understanding of the areas reviewed during the exam process, best practices, and regulatory requirements; exam questionnaires have been posted on NCUA's website. With full cooperation, the examination will be completed more quickly and keep disruption of the credit union's normal office routine to a minimum.

The examiner prepares and provides the officials with a written report highlighting the results of the examination. To derive the greatest benefit from the examination, the board of directors and committee members should review the report carefully. The board is responsible for taking necessary corrective actions, and the supervisory committee has the duty to ensure the board corrects identified problems.

The examiner will discuss problems and/or conditions which impair or may impair the safety and soundness of the credit union with the appropriate officials and employees. The examiner will also assist the officials with developing plans designed to overcome underlying causes of current or potential problems. Through conferences with the officials, the examiner will ensure they understand what must be done to improve operations. Officials can request a conference with the examiner in cases where the examination did not identify problems.

It is important to understand risk-focused examinations are not audits. The risk-focused examination objectives include determining whether a credit union is financially sound and whether operations are conducted in compliance with applicable laws and regulations. The *Federal Credit Union Act* places the responsibility for auditing the credit union on the supervisory committee.

Part II
Organizational Structure and Control

Membership

Eligibility for membership in a federal credit union is limited to the persons and organizations sharing the common bond described in the credit union's field of membership, as set forth in Section 5 of its charter. A person becomes a member upon approval of an application for membership, subscription of at least one share and payment of the initial installment thereon, and if required by the board of directors an entrance fee.

The members exercise democratic control of the credit union by attending and participating in regular and special membership meetings, and by electing the board of directors (and credit committee, if the Bylaws so provide). Each member is entitled to not more than one vote irrespective of the number of shares owned; and no member may vote by proxy, but a member other than a natural person may vote through a designated agent.

Regular and special meetings of the members are held in accordance with Sections 110 and 118 of the *Federal Credit Union Act* and Articles IV, V, and X of the Bylaws.

A member may be expelled from membership by action of the members or the board of directors as described in Section 118 of the Act and Article XIV of the Bylaws.

Board of Directors

The board of directors is elected by the members from the membership. They provide general direction and control of the credit union, and must meet at least once a month. The Act and Bylaws require the board to consist of an odd number of credit union members, not fewer than 5 nor more than 15. No member of the board may, as such, be compensated.

The board elects the credit union's officers, one of whom may be compensated, from its own number. These officers, whose titles are determined by the board, are the chair, one or more vice chairs, a financial officer, and a secretary. The board may employ one or more assistant financial officers, none of whom may serve as chair or vice chair; and one or more assistant secretaries, none of whom may serve as chair, vice chair, or financial officer.

The board of directors appoints the credit union's supervisory committee and, if the Bylaws provide, a credit committee or loan officers. The board may also appoint an executive committee, of not less than three directors, to act on behalf of the board and to carry out specific functions. No member of the supervisory, credit, or executive committees may be compensated as such.

The board may appoint a management official and one or more assistant management officials, none of whom may be members of the board, unless a standard bylaw amendment is adopted. These employees serve under the supervision of the board or financial officer and may be compensated. The directors may employ and fix the compensation of any other employees they deem necessary to carry out the credit union's operations.

The board may also establish committees from among the members to assist in the management of the credit union. Some committee examples include a budget committee, personnel policies committee, education committee, and delinquent loan committee.

For a full discussion of the board's responsibility for providing sound and effective management of the credit union's operations, refer to Part V, Management, of this Handbook.

Sections 111, 112, and 113 of the *Federal Credit Union Act* and Articles VI and VII of the Bylaws describe the duties and powers of the directors, board officers, and employees.

Credit Committee

In accordance with the credit union's Bylaws, the *Federal Credit Union Act* permits either the members of the credit union or the board of directors to appoint the credit committee. The committee must be comprised of an odd number of credit union members, not less than 3 nor more than 7. The committee is required to meet at least once a month.

The credit committee has the authority to appoint one or more loan officers, not more than one may serve on the committee. The committee may selectively delegate its powers to a loan officer and set the limits of the delegation. Applications or requests not approved by a loan officer must be acted upon by the credit committee.

If the Bylaws do not require a credit committee, the board of directors will appoint one or more loan officers and authorize them to assume the powers of a credit committee. A member may appeal to the board any application or request denied by a loan officer. Loan officers may be compensated to the extent authorized by the board. The duties and powers of the credit committee and loan officers are discussed in Section 114 of the Act and Article VIII of the Bylaws. Refer to Credit Services, in Part III, of this Handbook for additional discussion.

Supervisory Committee

The *Federal Credit Union Act* and the *Federal Credit Union Bylaws* stipulate the board of directors will appoint a supervisory committee consisting of not less than 3 and no more than 5 credit union members. One of the members of the committee may be a director, other than the financial officer of the board; however, no credit committee member or credit union employee may be a member of the committee.

The supervisory committee is an essential part of the credit union's management. Under the Act and Bylaws, the supervisory committee's major responsibilities include:

1. Make an audit at least annually.
2. Verify the accounts of the members at least once every 2 years. (Maintain record of account verifications)

The committee is also responsible for reviewing the performance of the officials and employees, and makes recommendations to the board of directors for improving operations within the credit union.

In order to carry out its responsibilities, but dependent on charter type and asset size, the supervisory committee may employ certified public accountants, public accountants, and/or other independent qualified persons to perform auditing, account verification, and clerical work under its supervision. The board of directors provides compensation to persons assisting the supervisory committee, but only the committee has the authority to select, prescribe the duties of, and remove such individuals. Refer to Part 715 of the *NCUA Rules and Regulations* for specific requirements.

The members of the supervisory committee are urged to study the *Supervisory Committee Guide for Federal Credit Unions (NCUA 8023)* for assistance in carrying out their important function.

Federal Credit Union Organization Chart

Members

Responsibilities:

1. Elect board of directors and credit committee.
2. Participate in membership meetings.
3. Promote participation in and use of credit union services.
4. Repay loans as agreed.
5. Remove any official for cause.
6. Expel members for cause.

Board of Directors

Responsibilities:

1. Maintain general direction and control.
2. Meet at least monthly and maintain minutes.
3. Establish operating policies and procedures.
4. Elect board officers and fix compensation of specified officer.
5. If bylaws provide, appoint credit committee or loan officer(s).
6. Appoint supervisory committee.
7. Appoint membership officer, executive and other committees.

Supervisory Committee

Responsibilities:

1. Make or cause to be made audits at least annually.
2. Submit audit reports to the board of directors and summaries to members at annual meetings.
3. Verify with members their account balances at least once every 2 years.
4. Maintain confidential relations with members.
5. Suspend directors, officers, or credit committee members for cause.

Credit Committee

Responsibilities:

1. Meet at least monthly and maintain minutes.
2. Appoint loan officer(s) as needed and delegate authority.
3. Counsel members in wise use of credit.
4. Maintain confidential relations with members.
5. Act on applications for loans and lines of credit.

6. Act on requests for release of collateral.
7. Act on requests for extensions and refinancing of loans.
8. Act on requests denied by loan officer(s).
9. Make annual report to members.

8. Hire, fix duties and compensation of employees and set personnel policies.
9. Maintain confidential relations with members.
10. Act on membership applications.
11. Determine classes of accounts and fix maximum individual share limit, when appropriate.
12. Fix loan policies regarding loan maximums, interest rate, maturity, and security.
13. Establish collection policies and procedures and fix late charges.
14. Designate depository for funds.
15. Authorize investments and borrowing.
16. Declare dividends and interest refunds.
17. Determine surety bond needs at least annually.
18. Authorize necessary insurance.
19. Provide necessary service facilities.
20. Act on loans to directors, credit and supervisory committee members in excess of $20,000.
21. Appoint a security officer and supervise security program.
22. Establish a records preservation program.
23. Request approval of charter and non-standard bylaw amendments.
24. Plan and hold annual meeting, report to members, and maintain minutes.

6. Call special membership meetings for cause.
7. Maintain committee's records.
8. Request board approval for compensation of clerical and auditing assistance.

Part III
Member Services

Thrift Services

The promotion of thrift is one of a federal credit union's basic purposes, and can lead to improvement of the economic and social conditions of the members.

In encouraging the members to save, a credit union may offer various share products, such as: Regular shares, share draft, share certificate, money market, and retirement plan accounts. Other less commonly used accounts include escrow, nonmember, and public unit accounts. A federal credit union must offer its members a regular share account, either as a separate account or in combination with any of the other available accounts.

Share accounts and share certificate accounts are the credit union's primary source of funds. A discussion of the different types of share accounts and applicable requirements can be found in Section 701.35 of *NCUA Rules and Regulations*.

Credit Services

Loans to members represent a federal credit union's major investment. The board of directors has the responsibility for setting written loan policies and is afforded considerable flexibility by Section 107(5) of the *Federal Credit Union Act* and Section 701.21 of *NCUA Rules and Regulations* on matters such as loan maturity, rate of interest, and security.

The provisions of the Act and the regulations, as well as of consumer laws and regulations, should be understood and followed by the board and credit committee/loan officers in their respective policymaking and credit approval roles. (Refer to Part VII for a discussion of consumer laws and regulations.)

The granting of loans by the credit committee and loan officers involves the three "C's" of credit. The three "C's" relate to Character, Capacity, and Collateral and are described below:

- A determination of character involves the development of information relating to the applicant's credit history. This may be obtained from other financial institutions and grantors of credit and from credit bureaus. The applicant's record of repayment of previous loans from the credit union is also relevant.

- In determining an applicant's capacity to repay, the credit committee or loan officer should carefully examine income, debts, debt payments, and living expenses. After debt payments and living expenses are taken into account, the applicant's income should be adequate to retire the loan in accordance with the agreed upon terms.

- Collateral is pledged security to which the credit union can turn for collection if the borrower defaults. The repayment schedule should provide that the loan balance is reduced more quickly than the collateral depreciates. The collateral should be readily convertible to cash. If the security is a co-maker, that individual should have the ability to repay in the case of default.

A federal credit union may grant unsecured and secured loans. Unsecured loans are consumer-type loans, usually relatively small, traditionally offered for various purposes incidental to the members' needs. Secured loans extend credit with a security interest in personal or real property of tangible value. The security may also be an endorsement by another person who agrees to repay if the borrower defaults. Co-maker loans, share-secured loans, and automobile loans are common types of secured loans. The following represent other types of secured loans:

Home Equity Loans: A home equity loan is designed to permit a borrower to make use of equity in the member's residence to increase borrowing capacity. It is usually secured by either a first or second mortgage on the residence. The maturity of a second mortgage loan is limited to 20 years.

Residential Real Estate Loans: A federal credit union may grant a residential real estate loan for a one-to-four-family dwelling, including an individual cooperative unit, that is or will be the principal residence of the borrower.

Maturity is limited to 40 years or longer as permitted by NCUA on a case-by-case basis. The loan must be secured by a perfected first lien on the dwelling or a perfected first security interest in a residential cooperative unit in favor of the credit union.

A sound lending policy stipulates written appraisals will be accomplished by independent, qualified appraisers be obtained on all loans secured by real property. Appraisal requirements are set forth in Part 722 of the **NCUA Rules and Regulations.**

Member Business Loans: Section 723 of *NCUA Rules and Regulations* defines a member business loan as a loan which will be used for a commercial, corporate, business, or agricultural purpose. However, the regulation exempts certain business loans from the member business loan definition. For example, a loan when added to other loans to a borrower or associated member (one with a common pecuniary interest in a business or commercial endeavor) totals less than $50,000.

A credit union wishing to grant business loans must adopt and implement the written loan policies required by the regulation and address the considerations discussed therein. Because of the risks and complexities involved, management should control the program carefully. The board of directors should determine the credit union's staff has the necessary credentials and qualifications, as outlined in Section 723, to grant such loans.

Lines of Credit and Open-End Loans: A line of credit is a fixed amount of credit agreed to by the borrower and the credit union. The amount may be drawn upon in increments or as a total. Repayment terms are contractually agreed upon and replenished amounts can again be withdrawn until the end of the contractual period. The line of credit may be secured or unsecured. Some credit unions fashion lines of credit in combination with home equity loans. Access to the line of credit may be permitted by different methods, such as checks or cash disbursements, automatic teller machines, loan drafts, and plastic credit cards. Because advances are pre-approved and readily accessible, line of credit borrowing is preferred by many consumers.

An open-end loan is similar to a line of credit plan. The primary difference is advances are pre-approved under the latter, while each open-end loan advance must be approved by a loan officer or the credit committee.

Guaranteed and Insured Loans: Federal credit unions may become qualified lenders under regulations established by various federal and state agencies. The agencies will either insure or guarantee loans made to credit union members for purposes provided for in the insuring or guaranteeing programs. The following list provides the most common guarantee or insured loan types: Real estate loans insured by the Federal Housing Administration (FHA), those guaranteed by the Veterans Administration (VA), student loans insured under the Federal Insured Student Loan Program, and business loan guaranteed by the Small Business Administration (SBA).

Financial Counseling

In today's complicated and competitive lending market, people are frequently tempted by easily obtainable credit. If credit is used wisely, it can enhance the quality of life and has contributed to today's high standard of living; however, if used unwisely, it can lead to impulse buying and overextension of credit.

Federal credit unions provide financial counseling services to assist members in managing their financial affairs effectively. The counseling program is usually under the stewardship of the credit committee or a loan officer. However, anyone having face-to-face contact with members, such as the financial officer or manager, may also be involved. Some credit unions engage professional consultants for this purpose.

Other Services

Federal credit unions provide other services for their members incidental to the basic purposes of promoting thrift and providing a source of credit. The ability of a credit union to offer such services depends on its expertise and its resources. Included among the services are the following:

- Electronic financial services
- Check cashing
- Sale of credit union checks,

traveler's checks, and money orders
- Trustee or custodial services
- Direct deposit of federal recurring payments
- Automated teller machines
- Sale and redemption of U. S. Savings Bonds
- Safe deposit box leasing

Refer to *NCUA Rules and Regulations* Part 721- Incidental Powers, for additional services with respect to pre-approved activities permitted to carry out a credit union's business purpose.

Part IV
Operational Requirements

Service Facilities

It is essential for credit unions to establish an office readily accessible to its members. If space is not provided by the sponsor, the board of directors should obtain conveniently located space at a cost within the credit union's ability to pay. The board should also provide for the necessary office furniture and equipment.

Land and Building

A federal credit union has the power to acquire land and a building necessary and incidental to its operations. Before making a major investment of this nature, the board of directors must develop a strategic plan outlining the need for the property and its effect on the credit union's earnings and overall financial condition. If real property is purchased for future expansion; it must be partially utilized within a reasonable period which shall not exceed 3 years, unless authorized by NCUA.

The purchase of land and building(s) is subject to the requirements and limitations set forth in Section 701.36 of *NCUA Rules and Regulations*. However, qualifying credit unions under the Regulatory Flexibility Program (RegFlex) are exempt from regulation 701.36 (a), (b) and (c) of this requirement. (Refer to *NCUA Rules and Regulations*, Part 742-RegFlex)

Branch Offices

The board of directors may establish one or more branch offices in order to serve outlying members more effectively. Prior to establishing branch operations, the credit union must ascertain the additional cost is part of its strategic plan and is affordable. Other operational details include: Implementing strong internal controls, centralizing recordkeeping, and establishing and maintaining a communication system between the branch and main office.

Office Facilities on Military Installations

A federal credit union with an office on a Department of Defense installation may have the option of using available space or constructing its own facilities. Authority for this activity is set out in Department of Defense Directive 1000.11, dated June 11, 2000.

Credit Union Service Contracts

A federal credit union may enter into a contract with one or more credit unions or other organizations for the purpose of jointly owning, sharing, buying, selling, renting, or leasing fixed assets or engaging in credit union services or other activities. For requirements concerning the terms of the contract, refer to Section 701.26 of *NCUA Rules and Regulations*.

Accounting System

The essential purpose of an accounting system is to provide a federal credit union's management with complete and accurate financial information it needs to make sound business decisions and conduct effective operations. The financial statements produced by the system are used by management to account to the members, creditors, and NCUA.

Credit unions under $10 Million in assets can use the *Accounting Manual for Federal Credit Unions* for information, guidelines, and recommended procedures and practices. Section 2000 of The Accounting Manual illustrates the prescribed accounting principles and standards which federal credit unions with under $10 Million in assets should follow if not using generally accepted accounting principles (GAAP).

In accordance with the *Credit Union Membership Access Act* (CUMAA), credit unions with $10 Million or more in assets must follow generally accepted accounting principles (GAAP) in the call reports they file with NCUA. Therefore, they should seek the advice of an independent accountant for guidance on full implementation.

Adherence to appropriate accounting principles and standards assures compliance with full and fair disclosure provisions of Section 702.402 of *NCUA Rules and Regulations*.

Employee Taxes

A federal credit union that pays salaries to one or more employees is subject to the provisions of law relating to withholding, remitting, and paying federal, state, and local taxes. For example:

    a. Federal income tax.
    b. State and local income taxes.
    c. Social Security tax.
    d. Federal unemployment compensation tax.
    e. State unemployment compensation tax.

The Internal Revenue Service's Circular E - Employer's Tax Guide, obtainable from the local district director, will be of particular assistance.

Worker's Compensation

Many states require employers to carry worker's compensation insurance covering employees against loss of earnings if injured on the job. The credit union should contact the appropriate state agency for information and instructions.

Surety Bond and Insurance Coverage

A federal credit union is required to obtain adequate surety bond coverage to protect it from direct losses resulting from dishonest and fraudulent acts of officials and employees and from losses due to theft or robbery. Part 713 of *NCUA Rules and Regulations* prescribes the required minimum bond coverage. The regulation also directs the board of directors to review and determine the adequacy of the credit union's bond protection at least annually.

The board of directors also has the responsibility of securing other insurance to protect the credit union's interest including fire, comprehensive, liability, and automobile insurance.

Records Preservation Program

A federal credit union is required to establish a records preservation program for the off-site storage of duplicate vital records which can be used for reconstruction purposes in the event of a catastrophe. The minimum requirements are prescribed in Part 749 of *NCUA Rules and Regulations.*

Security Program

Each federal credit union is required to institute a written security program in accordance with Part 748 of *NCUA Rules and Regulations* to protect the credit union from robberies, burglaries, larcenies, and embezzlements and to assist in the identification of persons who commit such crimes.

Part V

Management

The board of directors has responsibility for directing and controlling the affairs of the credit union and providing effective and efficient management of the credit union's operations. Accordingly, officials should develop a strategic plan.

Policies and Procedures

To carry out its responsibilities, the board should develop policies and procedures; and carefully design them to enable the credit union to function in a way to best serve the interests and needs of the membership. Comprehensive policies and procedures provide direction and instruction for officers, employees, and committees.

Written policies and procedures, at a minimum, should be:

1) Firm and clear in purpose
2) Consistent with the credit union's goals and objectives
3) In compliance with the *Federal Credit Union Act*, *NCUA Rules and Regulations*, *The Federal Credit Union Bylaws*, and other applicable laws and regulations
4) Based on sound and prudent business practices

Policy-making is a continuing responsibility; therefore, policies and procedures should be reviewed, evaluated, and adjusted at least annually. Any policy changes should be reflected in the board minutes. The board should maintain a "Policy Control Record Book" with a copy of each policy and showing the date of adoption and/or revision.

Program Management

Once policies and procedures are established, the board of directors is responsible for their implementation. To ensure proper implementation, the board should determine the following:

1) The person(s) responsible for carrying out the policies and procedures is aware of their intent and the expected results.

2) Each policy statement includes a periodic reporting or follow-up system so that the board can evaluate its effectiveness and amend the policy and/or procedure to achieve the intended results.
3) Coordination exists among the individuals assigned to implement the applicable policies and procedures.

To achieve the desired results in directing the credit union's program, the board should practice three basic principles of good management: Planning, Organizing, and Controlling.

Planning

Planning is the systematic arrangement of all the factors required to achieve the goals and objectives of the credit union's strategic plan. During the planning phase, the board should, at a minimum, answer the following questions:

a) What are the plan's goals and objectives?
b) When will the plan begin and end?
c) Who will implement the plan?
d) Who will monitor and report the progress of the plan?
e) Is the plan affordable?

Organizing

Organizing is the grouping of activities and individuals to effectively and efficiently accomplish the strategic plan. After the planning process has been established, the board of directors should mobilize, organize, and direct the staff and members who will implement the plans. The board should keep all involved individuals informed of the strategic plan's status.

Controlling

The board should control the activities and special assignments given, so it may readily determine if the strategic plan is being followed in accordance with established policies and procedures. Effective and continual program control by the board helps to:

- Prevent unauthorized actions that can hinder the financial growth and operations of the credit union.
- Keep members informed of the credit union's progress.

- Predict trends and forecast results.
- Make information available for evaluating staff performances.
- Provide data for considering new programs.
- Assess the effectiveness of programs to attain the credit union's objectives.

Administrative Management

Administrative management provides the internal controls necessary for operating the credit union's business effectively. It also detects and prevents illegal and unauthorized acts against the credit union. Internal controls are checks and balances built into policies and procedures. Many internal controls are developed out of daily experience and sound business practices.

Internal controls as prescribed by law, regulation, or sound business practice include:
(1) Dividing duties so that no one person has sole control over any transaction and its recording.
(2) Establishing the flow of work so one employee, acting independently, automatically verifies the work of another without duplicating work already performed.
(3) Providing physical facilities that support the maximum level of accuracy and work output.

To assure sound personnel and operational management, the board should establish the following:

- Personnel policies and procedures
- Position descriptions for all employees
- Performance evaluations at least annually for all employees (including top management)
- Training programs for officials and employees
- A screening process for new employees

Establishment and maintenance of internal controls in a federal credit union are the responsibility of the board of directors. However, the supervisory committee should review the credit union's internal control structure at least annually. The committee should report all weaknesses discovered to the board and then follow up to ensure identified weaknesses were corrected.

At least five types of internal controls should be utilized by the board of directors to assure maximum levels of service, growth, and protection for the members. They are organization, budgetary, accounting, methods and procedures, and auditing.

Organization

Effective organization provides for the logical delegation of duties, responsibilities, and authority, and should be adapted according to the size of the staff. The *Federal Credit Union Act* and the Bylaws establish the basic organization pattern for federal credit unions. As a credit union grows in size, further divisions of duties and responsibilities become necessary.

A credit union's organizational structure and procedures should provide strong internal controls, such as:

- Separate the duties of the loan approval process from loan disbursements.
- Assign the countersigning of checks and notes to a person other than a disbursing officer.
- Ensure supervisory committee internal audits are conducted completely independent of any official or employee.
- Segregate the maintenance of opening and closing accounts from those who handle the accounting records.

The Bylaws and the *Supervisory Committee Guide for Federal Credit Unions* contain information concerning organizational structure and internal controls.

Budgetary

Planning is an essential part of the budgetary process. Management should review economic conditions and all phases of the credit union's operations and should set long range objectives and short-term goals. Prior to implementing any new program(s) or project(s), management is encouraged to perform cost/benefit analysis and include all approved projected costs in the credit union's budget.

The final and most important steps are measuring the results against the budget, seeking explanations and understanding the reasons for variance, and making any necessary adjustments when warranted.

Accounting

A properly designed accounting system achieves sound internal controls and provides the board with reliable financial data. The actual results of operations should reflect whether a credit union is managed effectively and complies with board established policies and procedures.

Accounting control requires focus on the daily functions and operational aspects of the credit union, such as: 1. The proper methods for handling members' transactions and recording them on the books and records. 2. The receipt and disbursement of funds. 3. The preparation of financial statements which reflect the full and fair disclosure of the credit union's financial position and the results of operation.

Accounting procedures will depend on the credit union's asset size. Credit unions with less than $10 Million in assets should follow the *Accounting Manual*, Section 2. Federal Credit Unions with more than $10 Million in assets must follow GAAP when filing their call reports.

Methods and Procedures

To assure the business of the credit union is carried out orderly the board of directors should establish methods and procedures. When establishing methods and procedural controls, the board should apply the following principles:

1) Set fixed responsibilities.
2) Segregate duties so no one person handles a transaction from beginning to end.
3) Do not permit employees who receive and disburse cash to post to the members' ledgers. Also, do not permit them to reconcile the bank statement with the cash account.
4) Establish and use control devices on office equipment.

Require all employees, including the financial officer or management official, to take a vacation at least once each year and for an extended period of time not less than one full week.

A small credit union with only one or two experienced employees may face difficulty in following principles (2) and (3). To satisfy the checks and controls over daily work, the board must become involved. However, if this arrangement is not feasible, the internal auditing function of the supervisory committee becomes especially important. The supervisory committee should consider expanding the scope of its internal audit program to quarterly on-site reviews. An alert credit union management team continually studies its methods and procedures in an effort to make them more efficient, economical, and effective in helping to reach its strategic goals.

Internal Auditing

Internal auditing is the fifth type of internal control. As required by law, the supervisory committee functions as the internal auditing body of the credit union.

Each year the supervisory committee must perform or cause to perform a comprehensive annual audit. In addition, the committee is responsible for the members' account verification which must be performed not less frequently than once every 2 years. The *Supervisory Committee Guide for Federal Credit Unions* discusses the auditing and account verification procedures. The board of directors or the supervisory committee may not reduce the minimum standards set forth in the guide. However, they can expand the scope, the number of audits, and the supplemental procedures.

The supervisory committee must submit all audit and account verification reports to the board. These reports assist the board in evaluating whether the officials and the employees are functioning in the manner prescribed by the organizational, accounting, budgetary, and method and procedure controls.

By properly carrying out its responsibilities, the supervisory committee will help deter fraud, error, careless action, and willful violation of law, regulations, and policy. Although all fraud and error cannot be prevented, early detection can minimize reputation risk among the membership and the general public. Also, the financial officer or management official and the employees will normally make a greater effort to keep the records in proper order if they know the supervisory committee will quickly detect careless action.

Financial Management

Effective financial management is the basis for meeting sound financial objectives. In addition, effective management also balances the extension of credit union services with the achievement of safe and sound operations by properly utilizing credit union resources. The members receive a fair return in the form of well-designed services and reasonable dividends.

Financial management embraces a number of credit union programs. The following reflects significant credit union programs:

Share Program: Share and share certificate accounts are the primary source of credit union funds. Meeting the members' thrift needs is a major consideration when establishing share policies. However, the officials must also weigh the cost of funds and match shares with assets of similar maturities. For example, if long-term loans comprise most of a credit union's assets, share policies should strive to offer share accounts and share certificate accounts with extended maturity and restricted withdrawal features. On the other hand, if short-term loans comprise most of the credit union's assets, the officials might offer only regular share accounts and short-term share certificates.

The board must establish realistic dividend policies and rates. When setting dividend rates, the board should carefully consider the credit union's funding needs and the current market conditions. In the interest of sound financial management, the board should avoid paying above market dividend rates just to achieve rapid share growth. Rapid share growth results in excess liquidity which in turn can adversely affect earnings if the excess funds cannot be loaned out in a safe and sound manner.

At a minimum, the board's written share policies should establish the dividend periods, the dates the share deposits begin earning dividends, applicable withdrawal penalties, and establish the dividend computation methods.

Lending Program: A sound lending program is essential to the financial future of a credit union. The officials must strike a balance between meeting the members' needs and meeting the needs of the credit union's financial objectives and resources. The lending program should consider the credit union's share structure and funds flow, its short- and long-range goals and objectives, and local economic conditions. At a minimum, lending policies should clearly reflect maximum limits on loans; limitations on loan maturities and repayment terms; and acceptable collateral.

Loan Collections: Effective loan collection contributes to a credit union's ability to sustain loan services and to maintain a sound financial position; therefore, strong collection policies and procedures remain a vital part of the lending program. The board of directors should establish collection policies designed to keep loan delinquency to a minimum. Policies may differ from one credit union to another; however, a credit union's collection policies and procedures should at a minimum include the following:

- Follow-up actions for all delinquent loans.
- Accurate delinquent loan reporting to the board.
- Utilization of outside collection sources when internal efforts fail to produce results.
- Proper maintenance of collection records.

While loan collections may be delegated to a committee or staff member(s), the board has the responsibility of exercising close control over the program.

Investment Program: A credit union may at times have funds in excess of its needs. The *Federal Credit Union Act* and *NCUA Rules and Regulations*, Part 703 – Investment and Deposit Activities, provide guidance concerning investing activities. The board of directors is responsible to implement and monitor a sound investment program for their credit union. The scope of the program depends largely on the credit union's size, extent of its surplus funds, and management's expertise. A credit union's Investment Policies and Procedures should address the following:

1) Legality: The board of directors is responsible to ensure all investments comply with Sections 107(7), (8), and (15) of the Act and *NCUA Rules and Regulations*, Part 703.

2) Safety, Liquidity, and Yield: Sound investment policies assume a conservative ap-

proach in balancing safety, liquidity, and yield. In this context, liquidity means the ability to respond quickly to anticipated and unanticipated shifts in the credit union's flow of funds. Very often investments with greater risks command greater yields. Safety and yield should be carefully weighed prior to undertaking any investment that could result in a loss to the credit union.

3) Diversification: Credit unions can employ a diversification policy to minimize potential investment losses. Diversification of investments can minimize potential investment losses. Such a policy is particularly useful for credit unions that invest in marketable securities. The board's policies should clearly address diversification and specifically note any limitations it may place on the types of investments, quantities, and maturities to be purchased.

4) Accountability: While the board may delegate specific investment authority to an executive committee, an investment committee, or a management official; the board remains solely responsible for controlling the overall investment program.

5) FAS 115 - Classification of Securities: This accounting standard requires a federal credit union to classify its securities holdings (debt and equity securities) in one of three categories after assessing its intent and ability with regard to those holdings. The classification categories are: (1) Held-to-Maturity (2) Available-for-Sale (3) Trading. The related fair value of those securities classified as either Available-for-Sale or Trading must be assessed at least at the end of each dividend period (e.g., monthly, quarterly, semiannually, or annually). Sales and transfers out of the Held-to-Maturity category should be rare and any such transaction may raise questions about the appropriateness of the designation as Held-to-Maturity.

If the board employs a brokerage firm or other investment professional, the board must satisfy itself as to the reliability and financial soundness of the firm and the individual. Also, the credit union must retain discretionary control over the purchase and sale of investments. However, the regulation permits delegation of discretionary control provided the person is an investment adviser registered with the Securities and Exchange Commission (SEC), under the Investment Advisers Act of 1940. At the time of delegation, the amount delegated can not exceed, in the aggregate, 100 percent of its net worth. Annually, the board must review the delegation authority.

To determine whether to transact business with an investment adviser the board must analyze his or her background and information available from state or federal securities regulators, including any enforcement actions taken against the adviser or the associated personnel.

The board may not compensate an investment adviser who has discretionary control over the purchase and sale of investments on a per transaction basis or based on capital gains, capital appreciation, net income, performance relative to an index, or any other incentive basis. The board must obtain a report from its investment adviser at least monthly. The report should provide details concerning all investments under the adviser's control and their performance.

NCUA Interpretive Ruling and Policy Statement (IRPS) No. 98-2, dated April 1998, provides guidance for managing investment risks including market, credit, liquidity, operational, and legal risks. It also provides guidance on oversight of investment activities and describes, in general terms, the risk management process.

Additional information about federal credit union investments and related accounting procedures may be found in NCUA Letters to Credit Unions. Current investment information may also be obtained by using NCUA's Investment Hotline toll free at (800) 755-5999.

Borrowing: Borrowing is a means by which a credit union obtains additional funds on a temporary basis. If properly planned, borrowing can stimulate growth, help meet financial objectives through a period of tight money, and satisfy seasonal or other temporary needs. Borrowing should not be a substitute for an effective thrift promotion program or a stop-gap attempt to replenish funds.

The board may delegate borrowing authority to the executive committee, financial officer, or general manager. However, the board remains ultimately responsible for all borrowing by the credit union. The board should establish borrowing policies to include the following:

1) The conditions under which borrowing may occur
2) The amount that may be borrowed under each condition
3) The interest which may be paid on the borrowed funds.
4) The applicable repayment terms.

The board should coordinate borrowing and repayment plans with all other aspects of their financial management. For legal limitations on borrowing activity by a federal credit union, refer to Section 107(9) of the Act and Section 701.38 of *NCUA Rules and Regulations.*

Regulatory Flexibility Program (RegFlex)

RegFlex allows eligible credit unions to be exempted from all or part of specific regulations. Refer to *NCUA Rules and Regulations,* Part 742; for a complete list of exemptions. RegFlex eligibility is earned by credit unions who meet the following parameters:

1. CAMEL Composite of 1 or 2, for the past two consecutive exams;
2. and a net worth ratio of 9 percent or greater (or if a credit union is subject to a risk-based net worth requirement, net worth must be 200 basis points over its risked based net worth level or nine percent, whichever is higher)

The RegFlex exemption is usually automatic for those credit unions meeting both criteria. However, if a credit union meets only one criterion; management can apply to their applicable Regional Director for the RegFlex designation.

A credit union can lose their RegFlex eligibility if, at any time, the credit union no longer meets the criteria for the RegFlex designation. NCUA will notify credit unions if their eligibility has been rescinded. In addition, the NCUA Regional Director may revoke a credit union's RegFlex designation for substantive and documented safety and soundness issues.

Prompt Corrective Action / Net Worth

The NCUA Board prescribes to a system of prompt corrective action (PCA) to resolve the problems of insured credit unions. Complex credit unions are also subject to risk-based net worth requirements. *NCUA Rules and Regulations*, Part 702, defines net worth categories for purposes of PCA. The net worth categories include: Well Capitalized, Adequately Capitalized, Undercapitalized, Significantly Undercapitalized, and Critically Undercapitalized. The credit union's net worth should be sufficient to meet competitive pressure and adverse economic conditions as they arise, and should enhance the safety of the members' shares and keep pace with asset growth.

Funds Management

Funds management, also known as Asset/Liability Management, is the continuing arrangement and rearrangement of both sides of a credit union's balance sheet to obtain reasonable profits and provide for adequate liquidity and safety. It focuses on short-run adjustments of assets and liabilities to compensate for variations in the flow of funds. In the long run, a credit union's success depends on reconciling the different elements involved in obtaining and using funds. Since a credit union must have sufficient liquid assets to meet loan demand and share withdrawals, funds management policies and procedures are vital irrespective of the credit union's size.

The basis for applying funds management strategy is a thorough knowledge of the makeup of a credit union's field of membership; the nature of its assets and liabilities; and the economic and competitive environment in which it operates. Funds management techniques should be applied with a full understanding of the characteristics of the individual credit union. The following are considered essential elements of an effective funds management program: (1) Regular evaluation of the credit union's asset and liability structure (2) Regular assessment of asset yields and liability costs (3) Adequate planning for current and future liquidity needs (4) An on-going determination that policies are sufficient to efficiently structure assets and liabilities in order to meet changing economic conditions.

A necessary ingredient for sound financial management is a workable management information system. Reports containing basic financial information should be prepared and reviewed on a regular basis. Report formats and content will vary from one credit union to another, depending on the characteristics of each and its funds management methods.

The reports should, however, contain at least the following information:

1) Budgetary projections of income, expenses, and profitability.
2) Asset yields and liability costs.
3) Liquidity needs and sources of funds available to meet those needs, including the remaining maturities of all assets and liability accounts.
4) Economic and competitive conditions in the credit union's market area.

Financial Performance Report (FPR)

The FPR year-to-date data is derived from the credit union's quarterly Call Report (NCUA 5300). In addition to the year-to-date information, the FPR also presents the previous 5 years' financial performance in the form of ratios, statistics, and dollar amounts. FPRs also portray the credit union in relation to a credit union peer group of similar asset size. This is accomplished through utilization of peer averages and percentile rankings.

NCUA's *Financial Performance Report* (FPR) provides a long-term picture of the credit union's financial trends and operating results. The board of directors should use the FPR data to identify key trends, analyze past performance, and set future goals. A more detailed discussion of the FPR can be found in the *User's Guide for NCUA's Financial Performance Report* (NCUA 8008).

Part VI
NCUA Funds and Programs

National Credit Union Share Insurance Fund

The National Credit Union Share Insurance Fund (NCUSIF) was established by Congress in October 1970 for the purpose of insuring share deposits in member credit unions. Unlike the Federal Deposit Insurance Corporation (FDIC), the NCUSIF was launched without the benefit of appropriated or taxpayer monies. The Fund, an arm of NCUA, is managed under the direction of the three-person NCUA Board, and is audited annually by an independent accounting firm.

Share deposits in federally insured credit unions are insured up to the standard maximum share insurance amount (SMSIA), which is presently $100,000, an amount equal to the insurance protection offered by the FDIC. Generally, if a credit union member has more than one account in the same insured credit union, those accounts are added together and insured up to the SMSIA. However, there are exceptions to this rule including additional coverage of up to $250,000 for certain retirement accounts. NCUA Publication 8046, *Your Insured Funds*, explains the various types of member accounts and the insurance coverage afforded on each account, and answers questions most frequently asked about the Fund.

Credit unions which are insured by the NCUSIF are required to display the official NCUA insurance sign at the teller windows. All federal credit unions must be insured by the NCUSIF. No federally insured credit union may terminate its insurance without the written approval of the NCUA Board and an affirmative vote by a majority of the members. Sections 205 and 206 of the *Federal Credit Union Act* and Part 708b of *NCUA Rules and Regulations* spell out the exact steps to be taken.

The NCUSIF is funded through its member credit unions. Federally insured credit unions are required to maintain in the Fund a deposit equal to 1% of their insured shares. This deposit is carried as an asset on the credit union's financial statements and may earn a dividend if the Fund exceeds its normal operating level ratio of 1.30% during the insurance year. In addition to the deposit, an annual insurance premium equal to 1/12th of 1% may be assessed. Monies collected from credit unions are primarily invested in U S. Treasury securities; and the income earned is used to offset all administrative and insurance costs of the Fund. Any remaining income after payment of these costs is allocated to Fund equity to maintain the operating level ratio at or close to the 1.30% range.

The *Federal Credit Union Act* also authorizes the NCUSIF to grant assistance to problem credit unions in order to avoid involuntary liquidation. Under Section 208 of the Act, the NCUSIF may make loans to, purchase assets of, or establish accounts in such insured credit unions.

For further information about the NCUSIF, refer to Title II of the Act, Parts 740, 741, and 745 of *NCUA Rules and Regulations*.

Central Liquidity Facility

The Central Liquidity Facility (CLF) was created by Congress in 1979 because credit unions needed their own source of funds to meet their liquidity needs in the same way that the Federal Reserve System "discount window" provided access to loans for banks. Barriers to last-resort liquidity have changed favorably over time (e.g., credit unions who qualify may now borrow from the Federal Reserve discount window) but the CLF continues to be an important major back-up source of liquidity for both Federal and state-chartered credit unions.

The CLF is a "mixed ownership government corporation" within the National Credit Union Administration. It is an instrumentality of the Federal Government owned by its member credit unions and managed by the NCUA Board. The purpose of the CLF is to improve the general financial stability of credit unions by providing loans to meet unexpected share outflows, seasonal needs, and needs arising from emergencies such as strikes, plant closings, and local or national economic difficulties, when funds may not be available from other sources.

The CLF is designed to provide funds for liquidity purposes only, not to expand lending.

Membership is voluntary and open to all credit unions that purchase a prescribed amount of CLF stock. Additional information about the CLF may be found in Title III of the *Federal Credit Union Act* and Part 725 of *NCUA Rules and Regulations*. A credit union may also call the CLF at (703) 518-6620 with questions regarding loans and membership.

Community Development Revolving Loan Program for Credit Unions

The Community Development Revolving Loan Program for Credit Unions (Part 705 of *NCUA Rules and Regulations*) enables both federal and state-chartered credit unions meeting certain qualifications to apply for and receive loans of up to $300,000, in the aggregate, at a low fixed interest rate. The amount of the loan is based on funds availability, the credit worthiness of the participating credit union, financial need, and a demonstrated capability of a participating credit union to provide financial and related services to its members. Credit unions can apply by submitting a completed application to NCUA.

The Community Development Revolving Loan Program contains a matching component. Generally, the credit union must increase its share deposits in an amount equal to the loan. This requirement occurs within 1 year of the loan disbursement and the credit union must maintain the share deposit increase for the duration of the loan. Refer to *NCUA Rules and Regulations*, Part 705, for additional guidance.

Ombudsman Program

The duties and responsibilities of the Ombudsman (NCUA employee appointed by the Chairman and not in a program position) are to receive, review, and investigate external complaints of a regulatory nature unresolved at the operational level. Solutions are recommended since the Ombudsman does not have independent decision-making authority. Correspondence should be addressed to the Ombudsman, National Credit Union Administration, 1775 Duke Street, Alexandria, VA 22314-3428.

Part VII
Other Laws Affecting Federal Credit Unions

This part of the Handbook briefly discusses the laws and regulations, other than the *Federal Credit Union Act* and *NCUA Rules and Regulations*, which contain requirements which may affect the day-to-day operations of federal credit unions. The officials of a federal credit union have the responsibility of being aware of the provisions of these laws and regulations and ensuring the credit union complies.

Consumer Laws and Regulations

Truth in Savings Act

The purpose of the *Truth in Savings Act* (TISA), 12 U.S.C. 4301 et seq., is to assist consumers in comparing deposit accounts offered by depository institutions, principally through the disclosure of fees, the annual percentage yield (APY), the interest rate, and other account terms. The act and regulation require depository institutions to provide a consumer with disclosures upon request and before an account is opened.

This Act requires all credit unions to clearly and conspicuously disclose fees, dividend (or interest, if applicable) rates and other terms concerning accounts to members or potential members before they open accounts. The law also requires periodic statements be provided to members and include information about fees imposed, dividends (or interest, where applicable) earned, and the annual percentage yield earned on those accounts. Limitations on the methods used by credit unions to determine the balance on which dividends are calculated, and rules dealing with subsequent disclosure, electronic communication, and advertisements for accounts are also included in the law.

Truth in Lending Act, Regulation Z

The purpose of this regulation is to promote the informed use of consumer credit by requiring disclosures about its terms and conditions. The regulation requires very specific information to be disclosed for both open-end and closed-end loan plans. Credit unions that do not comply may be subject to civil liability as provided for by Section 130 of the *Truth in Lending Act*. This regulation is applicable only to extensions of consumer credit, i.e., credit offered primarily for personal, family, or household purposes.

Equal Credit Opportunity Act, Regulation B

Under this regulation, no creditor may discriminate on a prohibited basis in any aspect of a credit transaction. The prohibited bases are: race, color, religion, national origin, sex, marital status, age, receipt of income from any public assistance program, or good faith exercise of rights under the *Consumer Credit Protection Act*. The regulation addresses what information may be requested on loan applications, how it may be considered, and the content of notices required to be given following the action taken on loan applications. As with the *Truth in Lending Act*, the *Equal Credit Opportunity Act* contains a civil liability provision to protect the consumer against noncompliance by the credit union.

Electronic Fund Transfer Act, Regulation E

This regulation affords protection to members whose share accounts may be accessed through the use of an electronic terminal, telephone, or computer or magnetic tape, without the use of any paper instrument to initiate the transaction. The regulation requires disclosure of fees, terms and conditions applicable to such activity as well as documentation of such transfers and procedures for resolving errors within a specific time frame.

Preservation of Consumers' Claims and Defenses Rule

This Federal Trade Commission rule, better known as the "Holder in Due Course" rule, is intended to prevent sellers and creditors from unjustly separating the consumer's responsibility to pay for goods and services from the seller's obligation to deliver marketable goods or otherwise perform its obligations. It applies when the credit union is both the seller and the lender, as in the case of repossessed property sold to a member and financed by the credit union, as well as when the credit union has a formal or informal business arrangement with the seller to offer the financing on its merchandise.

Fair Credit Reporting Act

Credit unions are subject to the requirements of this Act when information obtained from a consumer reporting agency contributes to the denial of the applicant's loan request. The name and address of the reporting agency must be disclosed. When information obtained from a source other than a consumer reporting agency is used, the applicant must be told of the right to request, in writing, the nature of the information.

Real Estate Settlement Procedures Act (RESPA), Regulation X

To protect consumers, this regulation requires home buyers be provided documentation relating to financing and settlement costs of residential real estate transactions within 3 business days of submitting a mortgage loan application and at the time of settlement.

Home Ownership and Equity Protection Act (HOEPA)

This Act places restrictions on and requires disclosures regarding certain high-cost mortgage loans. It broadens the scope of mortgage loans subject to HOEPA by adjusting the price triggers used to determine coverage. It also restricts certain acts and practices in connection with HOEPA loans over a short period of time when the transactions are not in the borrower's interest. Finally, it strengthens HOEPA's prohibition against extending credit without regard to consumer's repayment ability.

Homeowners Protection Act of 1998

This *Homeowners Protection Act* is also known as the "PMI Cancellation Act." The Act addresses the difficulties homeowners have experienced in canceling private mortgage insurance (PMI). It also establishes provisions for the cancellation and termination of PMI and requires certain disclosure and notification requirements, plus requires the return of unearned premiums.

Fair Debt Collection Practices Act

A credit union is subject to this Act only if it regularly collects consumer debts on behalf of another party, with some exceptions. Various collection practices are prohibited such as harassment, intimidation, threats, and humiliation. If a credit union merely collects its own debts, compliance with this Act is not required; however, we recommend the credit union avoid those practices prohibited under the *Fair Debt Collection Practices Act*.

Home Mortgage Disclosure Act, Regulation C

This Act requires credit unions to disclose publicly where their mortgage loans have been granted. The purpose is to prevent lenders from ruling out or "redlining" certain residential areas of a city as ineligible for mortgage credit. The Act does not prohibit the creditor from determining the value of the collateral in relationship to the amount of credit requested.

Right to Financial Privacy Act

The *Right to Financial Privacy Act* protects the personal financial privacy of federal credit union members by restricting access to a credit union's financial records concerning its members.

The Act sets forth the conditions a credit union must meet before granting access to or before providing copies of financial records of a member to a government authority. In most cases, the credit union must obtain authorization from the member or secure from the government authority a subpoena or summons, a search warrant, a judicial subpoena, or a formal written request.

Under the Act, a credit union may disclose, to a government authority, the information it has relevant to a possible violation of any statute or regulation. Credit unions may give only identifying information and the nature of any suspected illegal activity. The Act provides the credit union or any official, employee, or agent is not liable to the member for making such disclosure or failing to notify the member thereof.

Soldiers' and Sailors' Civil Relief Act

Since persons entering military service sometimes do so at greatly reduced income, they may be unable to meet the terms of obligations they made while in civilian life. The *Soldiers' and Sailors' Civil Relief Act* provides protection during the period of reduced income. The Act does not cancel obligations but merely gives to those in military service who are financially unable to pay, protection against legal action to repossess collateral or force payment of an obligation.

The Act applies only to loans made prior to entering the service. It does not prevent a credit union from accepting loan payments or from continuing loan collection efforts short of legal steps.

The Act should be consulted for its application to the operation of a credit union. If any legal action against a borrower in military service is felt justified and necessary, the advice of local counsel should be obtained.

Fair Housing Act

The *Fair Housing Act* prohibits a credit union from denying a mortgage or home improvement loan to any member for reasons of race, color, national origin, religion, sex, handicap, or familial status (having children under the age of 18). Requirements and guidelines are set forth in Part 701.31 of *NCUA Rules and Regulations*.

Privacy Act

The *Privacy Act* protects individual privacy. The Act applies to the Federal Government's collection, maintenance, and use of information about individuals.

The *Privacy Act* may affect those federal credit unions whose sponsors are federal agencies or instrumentalities, but only in a limited way. While a federal agency (with the exception of agencies like the CIA) may routinely release the name, position, title, base pay, GS level, and duty station of an employee, the federal credit union may need to obtain its member's consent if it wants to secure additional information from the agency, for example, in connection with determining a loan applicant's creditworthiness.

Other Laws and Regulations

Bank Secrecy Act (BSA)

The *Bank Secrecy Act* includes several related Acts enacted by Congress, such as: the *Anti-Drug Abuse Act*, the *Money Laundering and Control Act*, the *Currency and Foreign Transactions Act*, and the *USA Patriot Act*. The primary objective of the BSA and its implementing regulation (31 CFR 103) is to provide a paper trail of financial transactions to help detect and prevent money laundering connected with drug trafficking, terrorism, and other criminal activities.

Credit unions must establish and maintain a written compliance program for fulfilling the requirements of the BSA that includes at least: (1) a system of internal controls; (2) designation of an individual to coordinate/monitor BSA compliance; (3) independent testing; and (4) training of appropriate personnel. In addition, an effective BSA compliance program should include written policies and procedures designed to detect and prevent money laundering activities. Failure to comply with the requirements of BSA and its implementing regulations can result in both civil and criminal penalties.

In its Letter to Credit Unions 03-CU-16, dated October 2003, NCUA provides guidelines to assist credit unions in complying with the BSA regulation. The letter also summarizes the recordkeeping and reporting requirements of the Treasury regulation.

Office of Foreign Asset Control Act (OFAC)

The *OFAC Act* requires credit unions to maintain a current list of prohibited individuals and countries. Also, the Act requires credit unions to compare their members, new members, and account transactions against the list, blocking all accounts and transactions with prohibited entities ongoing. To comply with OFAC, credit unions must:

- Understand the various laws, regulations and penalties for non-compliance with OFAC.

- Establish effective OFAC policies and procedures.
- Maintain a current list of prohibited countries, organizations, and individuals.
- Ensure the designated person compares and maintains the current list of prohibited countries, organizations, and individuals with members' transactions.

USA Patriot Act

The *USA Patriot Act* permits credit unions, upon providing notice to the United States Department of the Treasury, to share information with one another and other financial institutions in order to identify and report to the federal government activities which may involve money laundering or terrorist activity. Credit unions must ensure they maintain adequate policies and procedures to protect the security and confidentiality of such information. Also, credit unions may not use the shared information for any purpose other than what was authorized.

Section 326 of the *USA Patriot Act* sets forth minimum standards for financial institutions, including credit unions, for the identification and verification of the identity of any customer who opens an account. The written customer identification program (CIP) must be a part of the credit union's anti-money laundering program, approved by the board and should be tailored to the credit union's size, location, and type of business. Customers must be provided notice that the credit union is verifying their identity and why. The CIP must, at a minimum, provide for:

- Obtainment of certain basic identifying data;
- Verification of the identity of each customer to the extent reasonable and practicable;
- Maintenance of records of the information used to verify the identity; and
- Determination of whether the customer appears on any lists of suspected terrorists provided by the Federal government.

The CIP must also address:

- How to handle discrepancies in identifying information received;
- Terms under which a customer can conduct transactions while the identity is being verified; and

- What to do if the credit union cannot form a reasonable belief that the true identity of the customer is known.

At a minimum the credit union must obtain the following information prior to opening or adding a signatory to an account:

- Name;
- Date of birth (for individuals);
- Residential or business street address, APO or FPO or address of next of kin, (individual) or principal place of business, local office or other physical location (corporation, partnership, etc.); and
- Taxpayer identification number (U.S. person) or passport number and country of issuance, alien identification card number, or other government issued document bearing a photo or similar safeguard (non-U.S. person).

The credit union must retain records of the identifying information (name, date of birth, etc.) for five years after the account is closed. A description of the information used to verify the identity (driver's license number, passport number, etc.) must be maintained for five years after the record was made.

Gramm-Leach-Bliley Act

This Act requires credit unions to provide privacy notices to their members either at the initial time of establishing a customer relationship or on an annual basis for continuing customers. The privacy notice must be clear, conspicuous, and provide an accurate statement of the credit union's privacy practices. Furthermore, the notice should explicitly state the information a credit union collects about its customers, with whom it shares the information, and how it protects or safeguards the information. The Act also provides consumers an opportunity to "opt-out" of sharing their nonpublic personal information with nonaffiliated third parties. (Subject to certain limited exceptions) Refer to *NCUA Rules and Regulations*, Part 716 for more information.

Flood Disaster Protection Act (FDPA)

The *Flood Disaster Protection Act* of 1973 (FDPA) and Part 760 of *NCUA Rules and Regulations* prohibits federally insured credit unions from making, increasing, extending, or renewing any loan secured by improved real estate or a manufactured home if:

a) The property securing the loan is located in an area having special flood, mudslide or flood-erosion areas, as identified by the Federal Emergency Management Agency (FEMA)
b) The community is participating in the National Flood Insurance Program (NFIP)
c) Insurance is not purchased for the property securing the loan.

The principal objectives of the FDPA are to ensure that flood insurance is available at reasonable cost, to reduce or avoid future flood losses, and provide a preventive alternative to massive doses of federal disaster relief funds normally made available to flood stricken areas.

Bank Bribery Amendments Act

As required by the *Bank Bribery Amendments Act*, NCUA has established guidelines to assist the officials of federally insured credit unions in complying with that law. Consistent with the intent of the Act, to proscribe corrupt activity in credit unions, the guidelines prohibit any employee, officer, director, committee member, agent, or attorney from:

a) Soliciting for themselves or a third party (other than the credit union) anything of value from anyone in return for any business, service, or confidential information of the credit union.
b) Accepting anything of value (other than bona fide salaries and fees) from anyone in connection with the business of the credit union either before or after a transaction is discussed or consummated.

The guidelines encourage all federally insured credit unions to adopt written codes of conduct or policies explaining the prohibitions in the law. These codes or policies can desirably be included with those dealing with other areas of conduct such as conflicts of interest, discussed in Part VIII. Credit unions are urged to review NCUA Interpretative Ruling and Policy Statement No. 87-1, dated October 15, 1987, for a full discussion of the prohibitions and guidelines.

Government Securities Act of 1986

The *Government Securities Act* and its implementing regulations pertain to the following activities and duties of brokers and dealers in government securities: financial responsibility, protection of investor securities and funds, recordkeeping, reporting, and audit. The regulations also apply to the custody of government securities held by depository institutions. The Act does not significantly affect credit unions. However, credit unions who: (1) engage in reverse repurchase transactions in which they retain custody of securities subject to the repurchase transaction, or (2) offer members self-directed IRA plans in which the credit union will hold any securities purchased by the member, should consult the applicable provisions of the implementing regulations.

Abandoned Property Laws

Many states have laws requiring the transfer of inactive deposit accounts to the respective state. The credit union should consult the appropriate state agency regarding requirements and procedures.

Federal Election Campaign Act

The *Federal Election Campaign Act* prohibits federally chartered corporations (including federal credit unions) from contributing to political campaigns. However, the *Federal Election Commission Rules and Regulations* permit a trade association to solicit from a credit union's members if:

a) The credit union has separately and specifically approved the solicitation; and
b) The credit union has not approved a solicitation by any other trade association during the calendar year.

If these conditions are met, a federal credit union may disseminate to its members political information prepared by the trade association. Federal credit unions may not make share withdrawals for members for payments to a third party as political contributions. Doing so would constitute a donation of time and resources by the credit union and is prohibited.

Management Official Interlocks

Under the *Depository Institution Management Interlocks Act*, a management official of a depository institution or depository holding company is prohibited from also serving as a management official of another depository institution or depository holding company if the two organizations are not affiliated and are very large or located in the same local area. Part 711 of *NCUA Rules and Regulations* discusses the prohibitions as they apply to federally insured credit unions.

Expedited Funds Availability Act, Regulation CC

Regulation CC regulates funds availability policies, endorsement standards, and collection and return policies on checking, share draft, and other transaction accounts. It also establishes the date on which dividend credit must be given on a deposit item. Credit unions offering transaction accounts to members must fix and disclose their funds availability policies. The regulation provides specific timetables within which funds deposited in the credit union must be made available. All checks and share drafts must also adhere to a closely defined endorsement method. The placement and content of the endorsement are defined specifically in the regulation.

Part VIII
Conflict of Interest

Federal credit union officials and employees have an obligation to the credit union which extends beyond assuring that their actions do not violate any statute or regulation. Credit union officials and employees have a fiduciary responsibility to the credit union members to act in good faith in the performance of their duties.

In accepting a position as an official or employee of a federal credit union, an individual should recognize the interests of the credit union and its members have priority over any personal interest that individual may have. The position should not be used to gain personal profit or advantage. Acceptance of a position involves the assumption of fiduciary responsibilities, some of which are set forth in the *Federal Credit Union Act*, *NCUA Rules and Regulations*, *Federal Credit Union Bylaws*, and state laws.

Article XVI, Section 4 of the Bylaws provides that no official, employee, or agent may in any way act on any matter affecting that person's monetary interest or that of an entity in which she or he is interested.

NCUA Rules and Regulations prescribe the following prohibitions with respect to conflicts of interest.

Section 701.21(c)(8)–
Organization and Operations of Federal Credit Unions

A loan may not be made or line of credit extended if, either directly or indirectly, any commission, fee, or other compensation is to be received by an official, employee, or any immediate family member of such individual, in connection with underwriting, insuring, servicing, or collecting the loan or line of credit.

Section 701.21(d)(5)–
Organization and Operations of Federal Credit Unions

An official, immediate family member, or other person having a common ownership, investment, or other pecuniary interest in a business enterprise with an official or immediate family member may not obtain a loan or line of credit with preferential rates, terms, or conditions, or act as guarantor or endorser thereon.

Section 701.36(e)– Organization and Operations of Federal Credit Unions

A federal credit union may not buy or lease premises (with the exception of an informal lease maturing in less than a year) from any of the following without the prior written approval of NCUA:

a) An official or senior management employee or immediate family member of such person.
b) A corporation in which any of the above-named persons is an officer or director or has a stock interest of 10 percent or more.
c) A partnership in which any of the above-named persons is a general partner or a limited partner with an interest of 10 percent or more.

Section 703.120 – Investment and Deposit Activities

A federal credit union's officials, senior management employees, or their immediate family members may not receive anything of value in connection with the credit union's investment transactions.

Section 712.8(a)– Credit Union Service Organizations (CUSOs)

When a federal credit union has invested in or made loans to a credit union service organization, the credit union's officials, senior management employees, or their immediate family members may not receive any salary, commission, investment income, or other compensation from the organization either directly or indirectly, or from any person being served through the organization. The official or senior management employee may assist in operating the organization if compensation is not involved; the organization may, however, reimburse the credit union for services provided by the individual.

Section 721.7 – Incidental Powers

No official, employee, or their immediate family member may receive any direct or indirect compensation or benefit in connection with the credit union's engagement in any activity authorized under the Incidental Powers regulation. The prohibitions in Sections 712.8(a), 701.36(e), 703.120, and 721.7 apply to any employee not otherwise covered in the regulations unless the board of directors determines that no conflict of interest is involved in the respective cases. Where prohibitions are not specifically stated regarding transactions with business associates or family members, officials should exercise care to ensure such transactions are conducted at arm's length and in the best interest of the credit union.

Section 723.2(a) – Member Business Loans

A federal credit union may not grant member business loans to the following:

- Chief executive officer (typically President or Treasurer/Manager)
- Any assistant chief executive officer (e.g., Assistant President, Vice President, or Assistant Treasurer/Manager)
- Chief financial officer (comptroller)
- Any associated member or immediate family member of anyone listed above

Other

A number of federal criminal statutes apply to federally insured credit unions. Federal credit union officials and employees have the responsibility to report suspected criminal activities to the appropriate law enforcement agencies on NCUA Form 2362 (Suspicious Activities Report). Refer to Section 748.1 of *NCUA Rules and Regulations* for additional guidance.

The *Federal Credit Union Act* gives the board of directors responsibility for the general direction and control of the credit union. The board thus has the task of establishing policies and procedures for the conduct of the credit union's affairs, including the establishment and monitoring of investment and lending policies and appropriate dividend rates.

The board of directors should select competent management to carry out policies and procedures and monitor its performance. The board should strive to retain the best qualified personnel at rates most favorable to the credit union. While the salary and benefits offered to secure competent management will vary in each case, the directors should avoid contracts which might threaten the safety and soundness of the institution. Bonuses tied to increases in asset growth or income could have such an effect. They create an incentive for management to act in its own interests rather than those of the credit union.

The supervisory committee shares the board of directors' responsibility for determining that management practices are protecting the members' assets; that the board's policies and procedures are being administered properly; and that safeguards exist against fraud and conflict of interest.

NCUA encourages boards of directors of federal credit unions to establish codes of conduct to guide officials and employees in avoiding conflicts of interest. All should shun actions from which they would derive personal gain from the business of the credit union, other than normal salaries, benefits, and permissible non-preferential loans.

Part IX

Other Procedures and Supplemental Information

Mergers

Mergers of credit unions are usually effected for the purpose of continuing or improving service to members.

A federally insured credit union may merge with one or more credit unions provided they comply with the requirements set forth in Part 708b of *NCUA Rules and Regulations* and secure the prior approval of NCUA. If one of the credit unions is state-chartered, the merger must also be authorized by the state supervisory authority or permitted by state law. The regulation prescribes the procedures to be followed if termination of federal insurance or conversion of federal insurance to nonfederal insurance is involved.

NCUA publication *Credit Union Merger Manual* (NCUA 8056), provides required information and detailed instructions.

Conversions

A federal credit union may convert to a state-chartered credit union under the provisions of Section 125 of the *Federal Credit Union Act.* If the conversion involves termination of federal insurance or a change from federal insurance to non-federal insurance, the requirements outlined in Part 708b of *NCUA Rules and Regulations* must be met.

The Act also provides for conversion of a state-chartered credit union to a federal credit union and recites the relevant requirements. As pointed out in the Act, the conditions set forth in state law and by the state supervisor must be met in either type of conversion.

Liquidation-Voluntary and Involuntary

Should it become necessary for a federal credit union to liquidate, the liquidation is conducted in accordance with either the requirements of Part 709 (involuntary liquidation) or Part 710 (voluntary liquidation) of the *NCUA Rules and Regulations.*

The major responsibility of the board is to conduct the liquidation in such a manner which protects the interests of the members, the insurance fund, and the creditors of the credit union. If the board anticipates selling the credit union's loans but the bids of prospective purchasers will not provide sufficient funds to pay off shareholders at par, no sale may be consummated without written approval from NCUA. If the credit union becomes insolvent during liquidation, the NCUA Board may either provide assistance under Section 208 of The *Federal Credit Union Act* and restore solvency or place the credit union into involuntary liquidation and pay out the members, depending on the circumstances. The same alternatives apply when an operating credit union becomes insolvent.

Whereas a voluntary liquidation is conducted by a federal credit union's board of directors and shares are paid to members from the credit union's resources, an involuntary liquidation is supervised by NCUA and the members' shares are paid directly from the National Credit Union Share Insurance Fund up to the insured limit. Except in unusual cases, payout from the Fund is begun promptly following commencement of involuntary liquidation.

Credit Union Trade Associations

Local, state, and national trade associations promote the interests of the credit union industry. They offer a variety of services to their members, pursue the enactment and promulgation of, and changes in legislation and regulations, and represent credit union interests before NCUA, state legislatures, and the United States Congress.

The decision to join a trade association and approve expenses incidental to membership and participation rests with a federal credit union's board of directors.

Corporate Credit Unions

The *Federal Credit Union Act* authorizes federal credit unions to invest in shares, deposits, and certificates of corporate credit unions, federally or state-chartered. A corporate federal credit union is defined in Part 704 of *NCUA Rules and Regulations* as one that operates primarily to serve other credit unions and limits natural person members to the minimum required by state or federal law to charter and operate the credit union.

Corporate credit unions offer daily-balance share accounts which can earn dividends comparable to market rates offered by other financial institutions. Corporate credit unions also offer a variety of other investment accounts. In addition, many corporate credit unions offer accounts for clearing share drafts and credit card activity.

Credit Union Service Organizations

Credit union service organizations (CUSOs) are organizations that provide operational and financial services primarily to credit unions and the membership of affiliated credit unions.

The CUSOs in which federal credit unions may invest or to which they may make loans are limited by the *Federal Credit Union Act* to providing services associated with the routine operations of credit unions. The kinds of services they may offer are specified in Section 712.5 of *NCUA Rules and Regulations*. Examples are credit card services, automated teller machine services, and debt collection services.

A federal credit union may, by itself or with other credit unions form, invest in, or make loans to one or more CUSOs. Investment is limited to a total of 1 percent of the credit union's paid-in and unimpaired capital and surplus in the shares, stock, or obligation of the organization(s). Loans may not exceed 1 percent of the credit union's paid-in and unimpaired capital and surplus (independent of the 1 percent investment limit).

A CUSO must be structured as either a corporation or a limited partnership. A credit union must obtain written legal advice as to whether the CUSO is set up in a manner that will limit the credit union's potential exposure to no more than the loss of funds invested in or loaned to the CUSO. The credit union must, in addition, secure written agreements that the organization will follow generally accepted accounting principles; render financial statements and obtain a certified public accounting audit annually; and provide NCUA with complete access to the CUSO's records as deemed necessary by the NCUA Board in carrying out its responsibilities under the *Federal Credit Union Act.*

Part 712 of *NCUA Rules and Regulations* should be reviewed in detail before a federal credit union invests in or lends to a CUSO.

Member's Right to Inspect Credit Union Record

A member has the right to inspect a federal credit union's books and records, including the board of directors' minutes. The inspection must be made in good faith and for a proper purpose. It cannot be to satisfy mere curiosity or for vexatious purposes.

A proper purpose exists where a member is trying to determine the financial condition of the credit union or ascertain the manner in which the credit union's business is being conducted. Before making minutes and records available, however, the credit union must delete any confidential material that identifies the transactions of or personal information about other members.

National Credit Union Administration Publications

The NCUA publications referred to in this Handbook and other NCUA publications may be purchased from NCUA's Administrative Office at 1775 Duke Street, Alexandria, VA 22314-3428. The cost of a publication and a copy of a price list may be obtained by writing that office or calling (703) 518-6340. Many of NCUA's publications are on their Internet Web Site at *http://www.ncua.gov.*

Single copies of new publications and changes are forwarded to all federally insured credit unions.

National Credit Union Administration
Central Office
1775 Duke Street
Alexandria, VA 22314-3428
703-518-6300
www.ncua.gov

Regional Offices

REGION I (ALBANY)
Regional Director
National Credit Union Administration
9 Washington Square
Washington Avenue Extension
Albany, NY 12205
(518) 862-7400

Connecticut	New Hampshire
Maine	New York
Massachusetts	Rhode Island
Michigan	Vermont

REGION II (CAPITAL)
Regional Director
National Credit Union Administration
1775 Duke Street
Suite 4206
Alexandria, VA 22314-3437
(703) 519-4600

Delaware	New Jersey
District of Columbia	Pennsylvania
Maryland	Virginia
	West Virginia

REGION III (ATLANTA)
Regional Director
National Credit Union Administration
7000 Central Parkway
Suite 1600
Atlanta, GA 30328
(678) 443-3000

Alabama	North Carolina
Florida	Ohio
Georgia	Puerto Rico
Kentucky	South Carolina
Indiana	Tennessee
Mississippi	U. S. Virgin Islands

REGION IV (AUSTIN)
Regional Director
National Credit Union Administration
4807 Spicewood Springs Rd.
Suite 5200
Austin, Texas 78759-8490
(512) 342-5600

Arkansas	Nebraska
Illinois	North Dakota
Iowa	Oklahoma
Kansas	South Dakota
Louisiana	Texas
Minnesota	Wisconsin
Missouri	

REGION V (TEMPE)
Regional Director
National Credit Union Administration
1230 West Washington Street
Suite 301
Tempe, AZ 85072
(602) 302-6000

Alaska	Nevada
Arizona	New Mexico
California	Oregon
Colorado	Utah
Guam	Washington
Hawaii	Wyoming
Idaho	Montana

Index

A

Abandoned Property Laws	59
Accounting Bulletins	9
Accounting Control	35
Accounting Manual for Federal Credit Union, discussion of	28
Accounting System	28, 35
Administrative Management	33
Application for Membership	13
Audits, Supervisory Committee	15

B

Bank Bribery Amendments Act	57
Bank Secrecy Act (BSA)	54
Board of Directors - Powers Responsibilities	31
Board of Directors Election Directors, Officers, and Credit Committee	13
Board of Directors Meetings	13
Board of Directors	13
Borrowing by Credit Unions	40
Branch Offices	27
Brokerage Firm	39
Budgetary Program	34
Business Loans	23, 63
Bylaw Amendments	9
Bylaws, Discussion of	9

C

Central Liquidity Facility	46
Charter, Federal Credit Union	9
Committees, Appointment of	13
Community Development Revolving Loan Program (CDRL) for Credit Unions	47
Compensation of Directors, Officers, Committee members, and Employees	13

Conflict of Interest	61
Consumer Laws and Regulations	49
Controlling Credit Union Activities	32
Conversions	65
Corporate Credit Unions	66
Credit Committee	14
Credit Services	21
Credit Union Service Contracts	28
Credit Union Service Organizations	62, 67
Credit Union Trade Associations	66
Credit Worthiness	22
Currency and Foreign Transactions Act	54

D

Dividend Policy	37
Dividends	67

E

Election of Directors, Officers, and Credit Committee Members	13
Electronic Fund Transfer Act - Regulation E	50
Employee Taxes	29
Examinations	10
Expedited Funds Availability Act	59
Expelled From Membership	13

F

Fair Credit Reporting Act	51
Fair Debt Collection Practices Act	52
Fair Housing Act	53
FCU Act	7
FCU, Definition	7
FCU, Discussion Of	7
FCU Bylaws	9
Federal Election Campaign Act	58

Financial Accounting Standard - 115	39	**L**	
Financial Counseling	24	Land and Building	27
Financial Management	37	Lending Program	37
Financial Performance Report (FPR)	43	Letters to Credit Unions	40
		Line of Credit	23
Flood Disaster Protection Act	56	Liquidation-Voluntary and Involuntary	65
Funds Management	42	Loan Collections	38
G		Loan Officers	15
		Loans to Members	21
Government Securities Act of 1986	58		
Gramm-Leach-Bliley Act	56	**M**	
Guaranteed and Insured Loans	24		
		Management Official Interlocks	58
H		Management Officials	14
		Management	33
Home Equity Loans	22	Meetings	13
Home Mortgage Disclosure Act - Regulation C	52	Member Business Loans	23
		Member Services	21
Home Ownership and Equity Protection Act (HOEPA)	51	Member's Right to Inspect Credit Union Record	68
Homeowners Protection Act of 1998	51	Membership	13
		Mergers	65
I		Methods and Procedures	35
		Military Installations	28
Incidental Powers	63		
Insurance Coverage	29	**N**	
Insured Funds	45		
Insured Loans	24	National Credit Union Administration (NCUA)	7
Internal Auditing	36	National Credit Union Share Insurance Fund	45
Internal Controls	32		
Investement Diversification	39	NCUA Funds and Program	46
Investment Accountability	39	NCUA Letters, Regulatory Alerts, Interpretive Rulings, and Accounting Bulletins	9
investment Adviser	40		
Investment Policies	38		
Investment Program	38	NCUA Objectives	8
Involuntary Liquidation	65	NCUA Rules and Regulations	8
NCUA Interpretive Ruling and Policy Statement (IRPS) No. 98-2	40	Net Worth	42

O

Office Facilities on Military Installations	28
Office of Foreign Asset Control Act (OFAC)	54
Officers, Election and Compensation of	13
Ombudsman Program	47
Open-End Loans	23
Operational Requirements	27
Organization	34
Organizational Structure and Control	13
Organizing	32
Other Credit Union Services	24
Other Laws Affecting Federal Credit Unions	49
Other Procedures and Supplemental Information	65
Other statutes	54

P

Patriot Act	55
Personnel Policies and Procedures	33
Planning	34
Policies and Procedures	31
Preservation of Consumers' Claims and Defenses Rule	50
Privacy Act	53
Program Management	31
Prompt Corrective Action / Net Worth	42
Publications - NCUA	68

R

Records Preservation Program	29
Regional Offices	69
Regulation B, Equal Credit Opportunity Act	50
Regulation C, Home Mortgage Disclosure Act	52
Regulation CC, Expedited Funds Availability Act	59
Regulation E, Electronic Fund Transfer Act	50
Regulation X, Real Estate Settlement Procedures Act (RESPA)	51
Regulation Z, Truth-in-Lending Act	49
Regulatory Alerts	9
Regulatory Flexibility Program (RegFlex)	41
Residential Real Estate Loans	22
Right to Financial Privacy	52

S

Secured Loans	22
Security Program	30
Service Facilities	27
Share Policies	37
Share Program	37
Soldiers' and Sailors' Civil Relief Act	53

T

Thrift Services	21
Truth in Savings Act	49

W

Worker's Compensation	29

www.ingramcontent.com/pod-product-compliance
Lightning Source LLC
Chambersburg PA
CBHW070408230526
45471CB00006B/2704